# zen

## ***meditations***

### on being in love

# zen meditations on being in love

richard craze

MQP

# introduction

Love can turn your world upside down. It can strike out of nowhere and leave you reeling. Love can creep up on you slowly, quietly, until you suddenly realize the strength of your feelings. Or love can lie quietly like a sleeping cat, content and peaceful, secure in the knowledge of what it has.

Searching for love, winning love, maintaining love, learning to live with love, are all issues that are central to life. And how we cope with what is often the single most important relationship in our life has a huge bearing on who and what we are.

This little book of meditations is designed to help you understand the different ways love affects us, whether it is the thunderbolt out of the blue, or the gradual flowering of a precious friendship. Each meditation encourages you to consider, and to celebrate, the regenerative and transforming powers of love. By taking a few minutes out of the usual demands of the day to concentrate on the importance of love, and by learning to appreciate, and acknowledge, our feelings for our partner, lover, or spouse, we can learn better how to satisfy our own needs as well as those of the person most important to us. To aid meditation we have included a CD of music which has been specially composed to create an atmosphere conducive to contemplation. Use the CD in conjunction with the meditations in the book, or simply lie back and let your thoughts take their own path.

# the bond of love

## Live with me and be my love,
## And we will all the pleasures
## prove.

Shakespeare

To live alone without love is not living half a life, it is none at all. When two people meet and fall in love the two unite to become a single unit stronger and more powerful than the sum of their whole. When two people share their love and life equally and mutually there is a bond so close it becomes more than the mere meeting of two bodies, two hearts, two minds. It is the joining of two souls into one that has perfect understanding and yet the space and freedom to be separate.

# soul meets soul

Soul meets soul on lovers' lips.

Percy Bysshe Shelley

And as soul meets soul in perfect harmony love is formed, born, made, let loose on the world. When lovers kiss the world holds its breath and waits—waits for the release, the setting forth of the magic of love. Without the lovers, without the kiss, without the magic there would be just the cold gray dreariness of space. When lovers kiss the world is filled with color.

# love's fires

**Love is a log fire.** You cannot leave it to burn unattended or it will simply go out. It has to be cosseted and looked after. You have to provide fuel, to give it air and space and occasionally to clear away the ashes. A log fire has to be skillfully laid or it will not light—so does love. Too hasty and the whole thing will fail; too much air and it will not ignite; too little heat and it will remain cold. If a log fire, like a love affair, is tinkered with too often there is a danger it will fall apart and the hot embers be lost. A love affair, like a log fire, is best enjoyed by two people in comfort, sitting quietly enjoying the radiant warmth.

# invisible love

Love is one of those wonderful elemental forces like electricity that is so much more visible by its actions than its appearance. Oh I know you can see the vivid blue forks in a thunderstorm but that's an occasional thing. How much more wonderful to come home and flick a switch and have light and heat and power. And how much better to come home to warmth and tenderness. Love may be invisible but its effects are wonderful to see.

# the season of love

## Love, like nature, has its seasons.

In its newness it is like the summer sun—all heat and passion and ferocity. Then it cools a little in the fall rain, runs like a young child playing in the fields and woods gathering fallen leaves—it's all fun and harvest. There may be a winter season—cold and hidden. But you know the spring will come when there will be new growth, new life, new blood coursing. Then the fires will be lit again and love will return clothed anew in finery. It hadn't gone but was merely dormant, waiting, resting. And after each spring a return to the passion once more, the heat and the intensity.

# don’t question

# love

Don't question love. Don't try and tie it up in the interrogator's chair with a bright light on its face and a room full of detectives. It will simply plead ignorance of all your charges. "I?" it will say, looking innocent, "I know nothing about this." And in a curious way it will be right.

## Love has no reasons, no excuses, no plans, and absolutely no justifications.

It strikes where it will, when it wants, and at whom it may. We, the poor innocent victims, must only enjoy and accept. No, don't question love, it has diplomatic immunity.

# Love for love's sake not for what you might gain or lose.

Love for the look of a face, the movement of a heartbeat, the touch of a hand. Love for love's sake and not for how you might benefit or how much you might get in return. Love for love's sake and be happy to enjoy the moment with no thought of the future or the past. Spend each precious second appreciating and loving for love's sake.

# first love

## Remember your first love with tenderness.

Your first love teaches you so much, prepares the ground for the future and opens the gateway to adult love that will come later. First love is stung with freshness, laced with poignant fraught moments of uncertainty, and sudden unexpected passion. Never again will that exquisite love be repeated, its newness gone and its radiance dimmed with time.

# keeping wishes earth-bound

**When you love be realistic.** Accept what is there —don't wish for the stars when earth provides all you need. Keep your wishes earth-bound and you will enjoy happiness and peace. Raise your eyes to the heavens and you will be discontent, unhappy and restless.

# the truth of love

## What is love?

Is it the sleeping infant?
The bloom on a young girl's face? The confident stride of a young man? The tender holding of hands? An elderly couple content to sit in silence enjoying each other's company? Is it in nature? The first spring flowers? The beauty of a sunset? What are we to know of love? In truth love is in all these and much more. Love is the great unknowable. It is an experience to be enjoyed, taken while it lasts, savored for its moment of perfection—and then allowed to fall away naturally. The truth of love is that it is untouchable and unfathomable—we can understand nothing but feel everything about love.

Love is the wind that sweeps in from the east making us unsettled, restless, uncomfortable.

# the disorder of love

Everything we have known may be swept away and replaced. Love delights in disorder, it throws our normal view of the world out of the window, stands us on our heads and shakes us up to such an extent that we no longer know which way is north. And that's how it should be. Love is a disorder, a disease of the mind and an unsettling of the heart.

# the name of love

You can write love's name in the sand and the waves will wash away your proclamation in a moment. But the name will last forever. Once the sand has been disturbed by your writing it will never settle again exactly the way it was, with the same rhythm, the same granulation. Again and again you can write it and always the tide will play with your efforts.

Love may die and settle like the sand but its memory lingers on for all eternity.

# evocations of love

## Once there was no scent, nothing, no smell on the air.

Then love came and everything bloomed into the sweet, heady scent of delight. Roses magnified their smell and sweet honeysuckle blew its charge into the evening air. Nothing is the same again. Love changes the air around us, transforms it with sweet perfume that brings memories and moments back to us in heart-stopping evocation.

# love knows

When we have to question, ask, analyze, then love isn't there.

## When love is there, we have no questions.

Love knows, so we know. Love is strength, conviction, complete knowing. Love is complete and will not be asked if it is real. Love is sure knowledge, and its knowing is all encompassing, all encircling, all surrounding. When love knows, we are certain.

the moment of love

In a look it is understood—love is. There is no mistake, no doubting. In that one quick moment of utter knowing, love blooms instantly into all time, all space. In that one look love is born and will not die. Love can be changed and transformed, modified and played with—but never killed. It cannot die. In an instant love is brought into the world and, once created, lives on. The moment of love is immortal—love is forever.

# love's energy

## The force that is love waits in our heart for the right moment to show itself.

It is all energy, all passion, all movement. It can only reveal itself through the outline, the shape, the guise of another. Through your eyes I see love in your heart and your soul. It is not the true shape of love, which is just energy, but through you I can see love. I honor the love in you, through you, because of you.

# love is ...

Love is an empty room when you are not there. Love is a cold bed when you are away. Love is the silence when we do not speak. Love is my hand closing on empty air when your hand is drawn away. Love is a cold kiss on cold air when your lips are not there. Love is a dark shadow when you are not there to animate it, bring warmth and life and color to it. Love is nothing when you are not around.

# the passage of love

## The river flows toward the sea and crosses many landscapes. So it is with love.

The river crosses mudflats and shingle shores, grassy banks and shadowy backwaters. It flows down tumultuous weirs and waterfalls, enjoys slow meanders of quiet sunshine and even changes course and direction. But always it is the river and always it flows to the sea. It doesn't judge its passage. The same should be true of our love. At times it will be stormy and wild and at others calm and gentle. But always it is our love and always we are moving in the right direction.

# love's choice

## I did not choose. I had no control.

I did nothing to create this. I was passive. I stood by while this process was begun, given life and shape, brought forth, born and grew. I had no choice. My love chose, had its own election, cast its vote, ticked the ballot paper with your name on it. I did not choose but my love was absolutely right and you are elected.

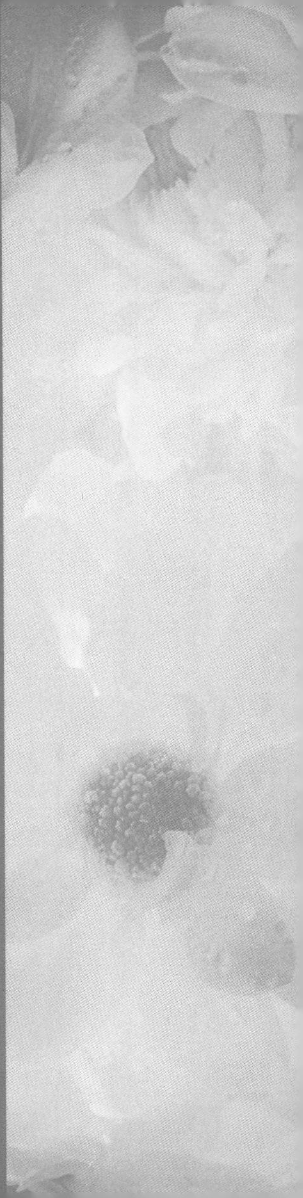

# the cosmic dance

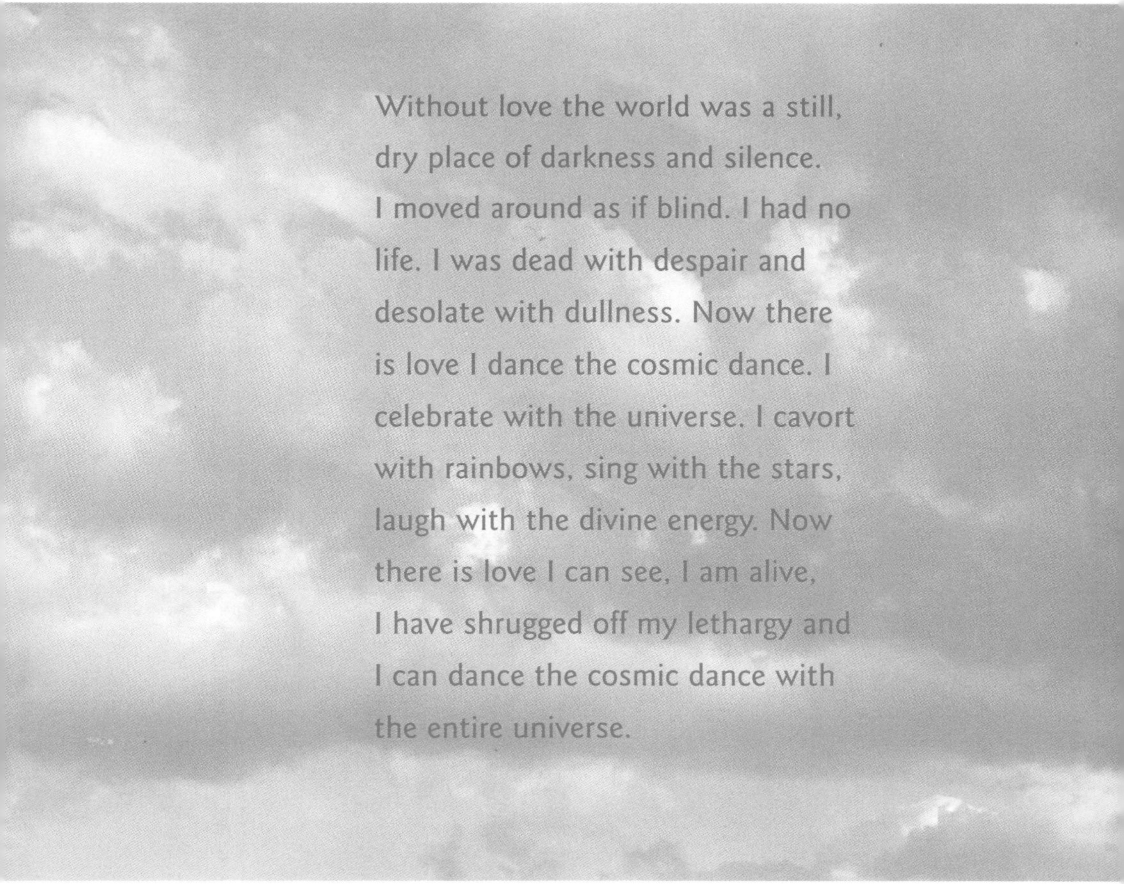

Without love the world was a still, dry place of darkness and silence. I moved around as if blind. I had no life. I was dead with despair and desolate with dullness. Now there is love I dance the cosmic dance. I celebrate with the universe. I cavort with rainbows, sing with the stars, laugh with the divine energy. Now there is love I can see, I am alive, I have shrugged off my lethargy and I can dance the cosmic dance with the entire universe.

love is more

We think we know so much about love. We meet and surrender, seduce and woo. We marry and settle, breed and grow old. All in the space of the twinkle of an eye. But what is this thing called love to be squandered so? To be so lightly toyed with and tossed aside into the humdrum routine of our existence? Love is universal, bigger than time and space, greater than the sum of all of humanity's achievements. And we lose it in the normality of our daily lives. Love is too big, too grand to be wasted on the everyday predictability of our lives. Love is vast and transforming, and we try to cram it into a tiny corner of our life. Love is more.

# the simplicity of love

## A Book of Verses underneath the Bough.
## A Jug of Wine, a Loaf of Bread—and Thou.

*The Rubaiyat*, Omar Khayyam

Love doesn't need fanfares and parades, expensive suits or gold jewelry. Love is as happy with a simple meal as a banquet. The music of love is played as well on a simple wooden flute as with the massed strings and instruments of an orchestra. Love is a simple poem and not a complete library. Love is lost in the city streets and found in a quiet field or wood dappled with sunlight. Love is two people sharing simplicity, not a crowd surging forward. Love is a quiet moment of contemplation and its voice is serene and still. Love is simplicity.

# my love is come to me

My heart is like a singing bird
Whose nest is in a watered shoot;
My heart is like an apple tree
Whose boughs are bent with thickset fruit;
My heart is like a rainbow shell
That paddles in a halcyon sea;
My heart is gladder than all these
Because my love is come to me.

"A Birthday," Christina Rossetti

# the contemplation

Even sitting here in the cool silence, in the contemplation of meditation I can discover the universe, see its infinite tricks and diversions, experience the oneness of the cosmos, play in the divinity of the spirit.

## But I cannot experience Love.

To do that I have to get up, pack up my meditation blanket and walk out into the real world. There, moving amongst real people, I may experience it. In the blessed peace of my mantra I may understand the universal love, the true pure love of God, but to experience the love of person to person I have no choice but to be out in the world participating, talking, moving, dancing, living.

# the patience of love

## Be patient with your love.

Treat them as you would your best friend. Give them the time and space to be themselves and not only what you want them to be. Be patient with your love and allow them to blossom and grow, and your love will thrive with them. Be there to support them when they need you, and be their strength, and be vulnerable enough to show them how much you need them in return.

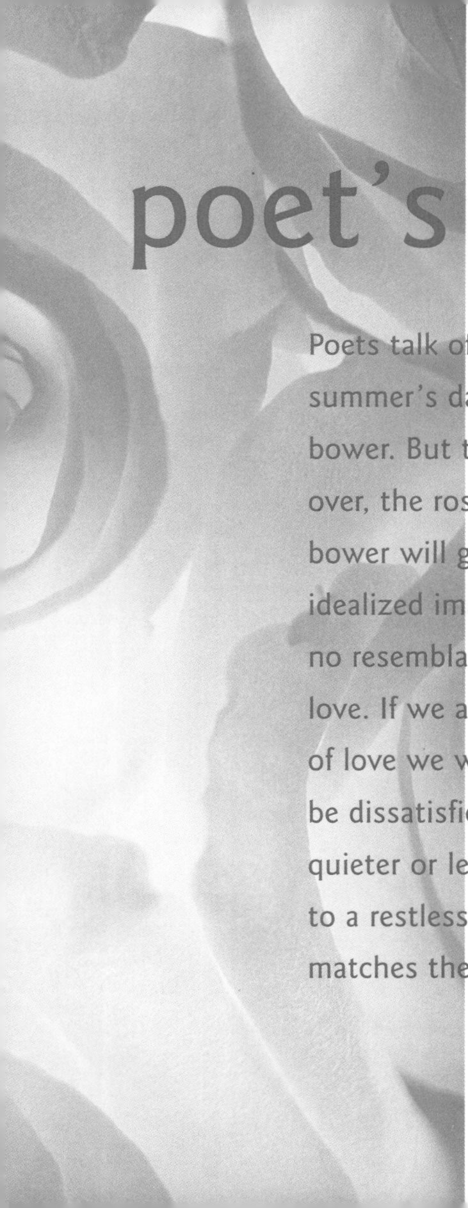

# poet's love

Poets talk of love and compare it to a summer's day, or a rose, or a moonlit bower. But the summer's day will cloud over, the rose has thorns, and the moonlit bower will grow cold and dark. The idealized images that poets conjure up bear no resemblance to real, living, breathing love. If we are seduced by the poet's image of love we will expect the impossible, and be dissatisfied if our love is smaller or quieter or less exotic. The poet's love leads to a restless place where nothing quite matches the vision of perfection.

Love cannot be seen, but it can be felt, it has no substance and yet it is one of the most powerful forces that plays on our lives.

Love has the transforming energy to take the ordinary, the mundane and the trivial, and elevate them to the extraordinary, the incredible, the startlingly significant. When love touches our lives it seems gentle, and yet it has the strength to turn everything we know and accept upside down in an instant—with the merest glance of an eye or the touch of a hand.

# the power of love

I love you

I love you in all your different moods.

I love the way your eyes suddenly fill with anger, or tears, or wrinkle up with laughter. I love the way you try to catch me off guard, to ask about my past, to treat me unkindly. I love the way you refuse me. I love the way you keep yourself separate from me, and yet come to me for love. I love the way you rebel and stamp your feet. I love the way you hate to be loved. I love you in all your wiles and guiles and subterfuges. I love your taste and smell and touch.

I love you very much

# as you are

I don't want you for anything but what you are. I don't want to change you because, in changing, the love we have will evaporate. I love you for you right now, right here. I love you exactly as you are with no hint of imperfection in all your imperfections. I love you, not for what you can do, or say, or be, but for what you are. I love you for how you are. I love you now for when you are.

This time is right and I love you as you are.

Love is elusive and mysterious.

# don't look for love

## Love is elusive and mysterious.

It seeks us out when we least expect it. If we go looking for Love it will hide. If we try to draw Love out it will become more entrenched. If we don't look for Love it will find us. If we don't look for Love it will be intrigued and find a way into our hearts.

# an open heart

Love is an open heart full of forgiveness. Love is not bound by rules or judgments, morals or orders. Love is an open heart full of giving, without seeking a return on investment or a capital pay off. Love is an open heart with the enthusiasm of a small child, the innocence of kittens, and the smile of a baby. Love is an open heart with joy, grace, and beauty. Love is an open heart that welcomes you in, no matter what.

**Love is an open heart.**

and in time let go

For this is wisdom; to love, to live,
To take what fate, or the gods, may give,
To ask no question, to make no prayer,
But to kiss the lips and caress the hair,
Speed passion's ebb as you greet its flow,—
To have,—to hold,—and,—in time—let go.

Laurence Hope

# social conscience

# Love has no social conscience.

It is available to kings and beggars, the rich and the poor, the good and the wicked, the kind and the cruel. Tyrants are just as likely to be afflicted as the innocence of youth. Love doesn't keep score of your misdeeds or how much you gave to charity. Love knows no boundaries or borders.

## Love has no reason or rules and will strike where it fancies without thought of the consequences.

Love is irrational—we are as likely to suffer love as to benefit from it. It is indiscriminate and exciting, haphazard and scintillating, random and interesting. Love is never dull or predictable.

When we lovers reach out for each other we touch without words. We hold hands in silence or we talk of other things. In the dark night when we caress we do so with sighs and whispers, kisses, and breathy exhalations of love. We are in love with each other, and this is what it is like, or what it is like in words.

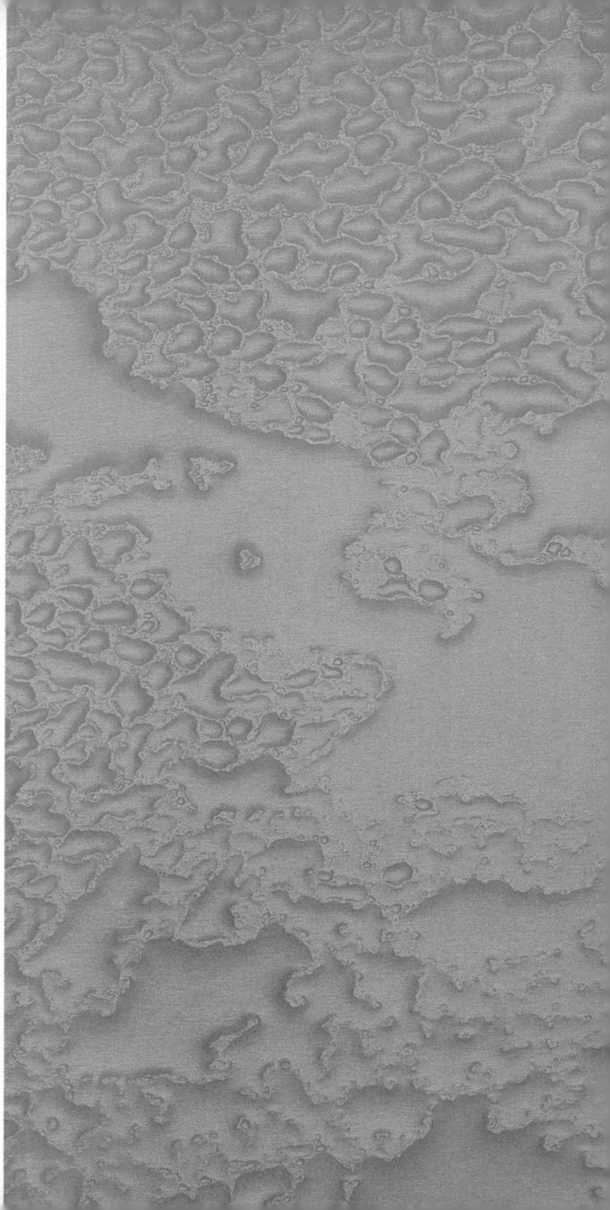

# love in words

# love's sweet music

Love is not in the individual notes
but in the air vibrating, in the complexity
of the sounds poured together.

Love is the strings of a violin waiting to be played. Together the strings will make great music if played expertly. If jangled by an inexperienced player the sound can be harsh and inharmonious. But played well the strings sing with melody and sing together, sing well and vibrate with harmony. Love the unwritten music, the elation in the mood of the listener, the magic of the spell.

love's time dying

Already, before the instant has passed,
love's time is dying. Fading to dust even
as it is born. Love is too precious, too sweet.
Too exquisitely fragile to last. It will die on the
morning light and be blown away with dawn's
gentle breeze. The time of love is passing
and we must appreciate it with every second.
In its delicate birth its seeds of death
are already sown.

# the amount of love

When we are young we love our parents, our siblings, our grandparents—even a favorite toy. As we grow older we love our partner and our children, our friends and our partner's parents and siblings. Older still and we have our grandchildren to love as well. There is no limit to the amount of love we have to give—and no limit to the number of people we have to give that love to.

# I know nothing of love

When I was a child I thought I knew love. It was all holding hands and crying at the moon. When I was young I was confident in love. It was all wooing and passion and bringing flowers. When I was fully grown I was sure I knew love. It was all babies and being together. Now I am old I am convinced I know love. It is all comfort and nurturing each other, looking back with fondness and memories.

But in all this, the love I know for you changes shape every day, eludes my grasp with its newness and challenges my intellect with its depths of feeling. I now know I know nothing of love—except its divine experience.

the hours
spent loving

## The Gods do not deduct from one's life the hours spent loving.

Ancient Chinese proverb

And if the Gods don't, why should we? Hours spent loving are outside the normal jurisdiction of our lives, unlike work, or chores, or being angry. The hours spent loving are sacred and operate in their own magical atmosphere of enchantment and divinity, and when we return to the real world we perceive it as a dream, and realize the hours spent loving were the reality that we have moved away from.

# giving love space

Give love space and it will grow. Give your partner time and growing room and they will flourish. Cramp them and they will wither. Love needs a time to come together and a time for being apart. It was your partner's heart you fell in love with, not their living room. It was for the radiance of their face and not their house you first felt the stirrings of desire. Hearts may be joined but not tents. Tents are for going to, to recuperate, to have space, to rest and think.
Give each other space and you
will come back together
stronger and more
able to love.

Keep your hearts together,
but your tents separate.

Bedouin proverb

# guilty of dust and sin

Love bade me welcome; yet my soul drew back,
Guilty of dust and sin.

"Love," George Herbert

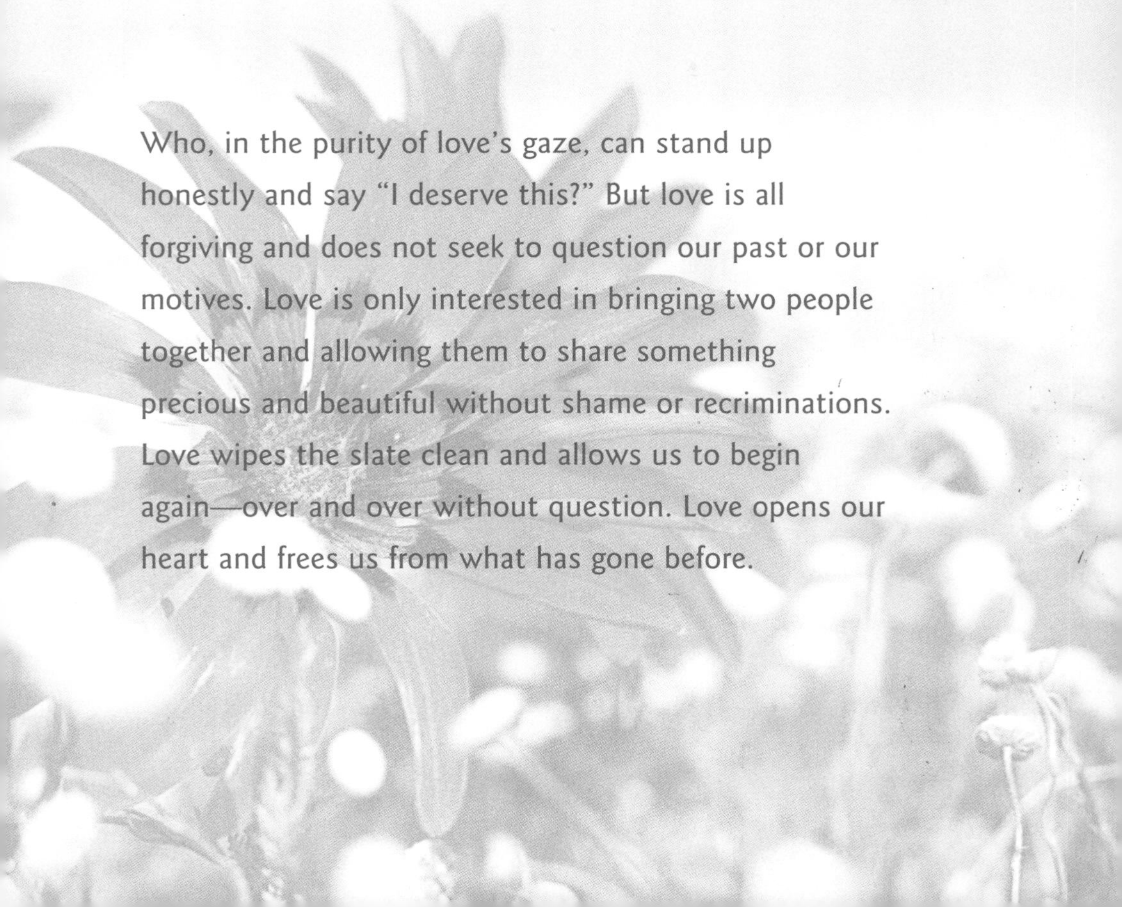

Who, in the purity of love's gaze, can stand up honestly and say "I deserve this?" But love is all forgiving and does not seek to question our past or our motives. Love is only interested in bringing two people together and allowing them to share something precious and beautiful without shame or recriminations. Love wipes the slate clean and allows us to begin again—over and over without question. Love opens our heart and frees us from what has gone before.

# the inspiration of love

## Love is the greatest inspiration of all.

It can make us do the impossible, the fantastic, the dangerous, the reckless, and the perilous. It can make us screw up our courage in both hands and take blind leaps of faith into the darkness of the future. For love we will dare anything. For love we will stand alone against overwhelming odds. For love we will lay down our lives gladly and without thought. For love we would risk everything. Love is an inspiration beyond all other.

# the soothing song of love

In times of trouble, love has an ability to soothe away our fears, to comfort us, to nurse us back to health. Love can enter our coma and bring us back to life. Love can soothe away our worst nightmares, soothe away our tears, soothe away our pain. Love heals without medicine or therapy.

Love soothes with a sweet song that has no words or music.

# the acceptance of love

Love wants to change nothing. Love accepts us as we are. Love is not love if it seeks to improve, to alter, to transform, to modify, or convert. Love is blind to our faults and our virtues alike. Love is acceptance and wants only to be experienced and not to be a catalyst for improvement. Love is the acceptance that love is—

nothing more,

nothing less.

Love is the acceptance that love is

trust in love

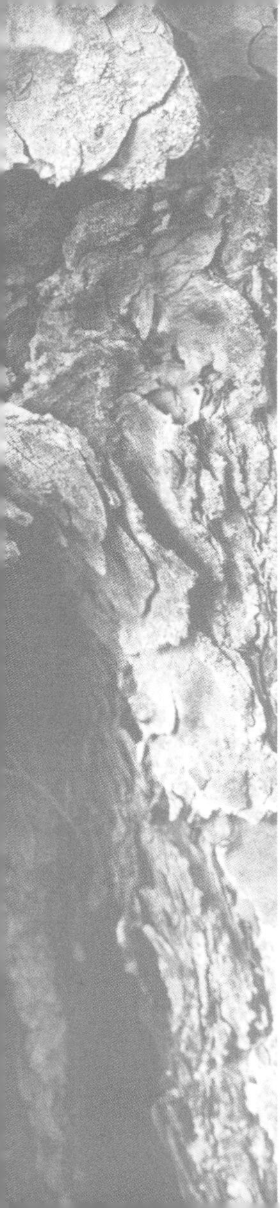

When we fall in love we find in that other person all our hopes and dreams. We look to them to help us discover and explore our potential. And of course we also seek to possess them. This isn't love, it is ownership and, as such, not a true part of love at all. Naturally we want our love to give us the best of themselves. If we see them give more to others we will be jealous. But if we trust in love we can share them with others and enjoy their freedom and independence.

## We have to trust in love for love to flourish.

# love's beginnings

Who can say when love begins? Who can predict that the
first touch of hand on hand will lead to such intensity?
If we could predict, would we draw back from such a touch?
Who can say when love begins? Is it in a look or a glance,
a touch or a kiss? We all know when and
how love dies and can feel its
pain in all its ferocity.
But who can say
when love begins?

# If we are to be loved we must give love.

If we are to give love we must be capable of receiving love. The more open our hearts are to love the more we have to share ourselves. The more we give our love away the more it returns. Love doubles in giving and doubles in receiving. Love goes toward love. Love attracts itself over and over again. If we are unloved it is into our own hearts we must first look for the fault and not at others. If we cannot give love it is again into our own heart we must look.

**The more we love the more love we will have to give and receive.**

love goes
towards love

# love's passion dims

Everything has a season, a time, a perfect way to be. So it is with love. **Love is a calendar of time.**

It begins each new month, year, century, full of hope and bright vitality, and it is spent by the time it runs its course, grown old and weary with acquaintance. Then you turn the page, rip off another diary date and love springs anew. Love is a fresh page waiting to be written on with words of endearment and encouragement. Love's passion dims when the page reaches its end but is always ready to be reprinted with new energy and life once we learn the trick of tearing off the old and seeing the new.

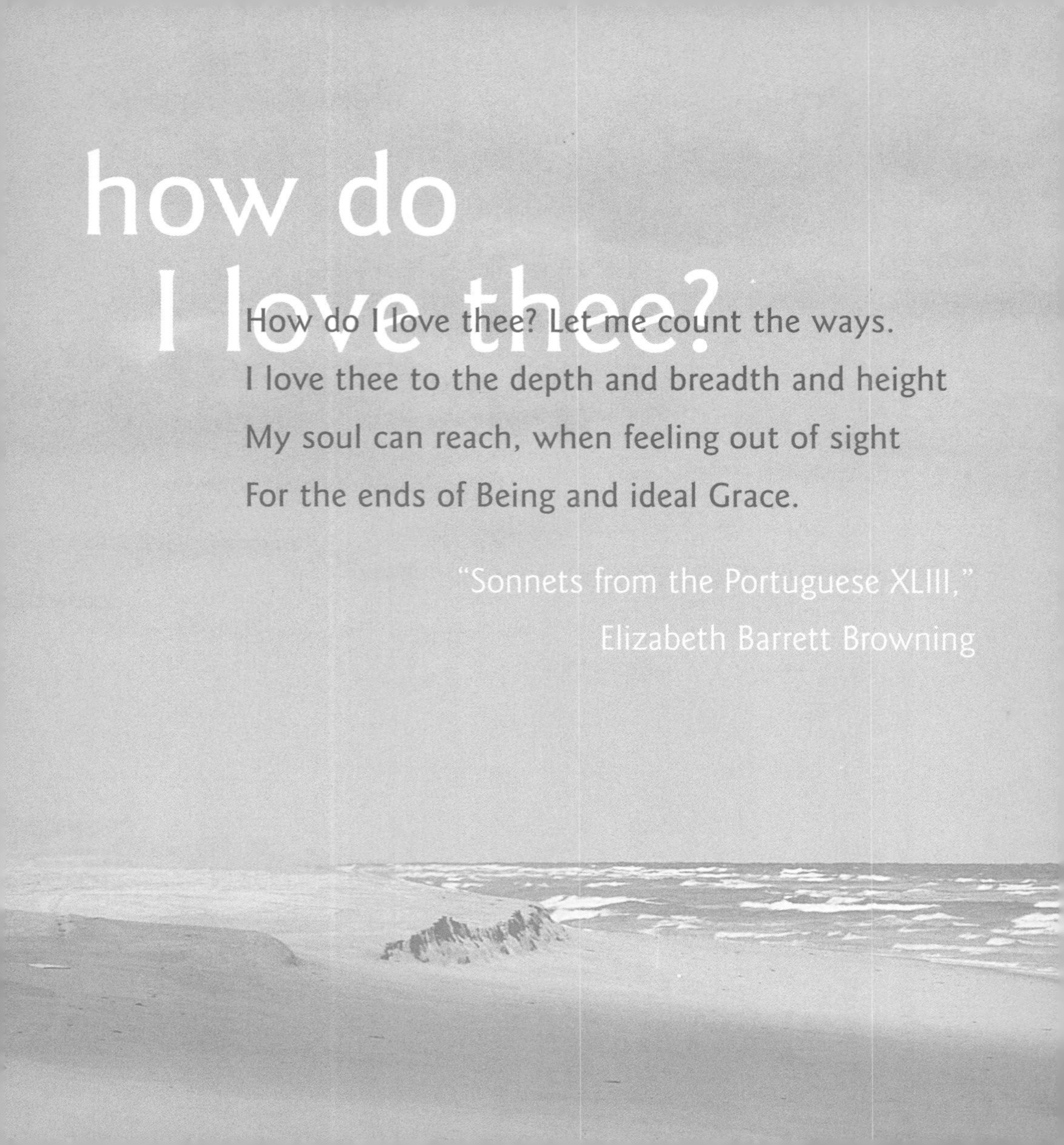

# how do I love thee?

How do I love thee? Let me count the ways.
I love thee to the depth and breadth and height
My soul can reach, when feeling out of sight
For the ends of Being and ideal Grace.

"Sonnets from the Portuguese XLIII,"
Elizabeth Barrett Browning

To love is to explore the depths of our being, our soul, our very existence. To be loved is to share and experience that with another person. This unique glimpse into another's soul is precious, must be treated with the utmost respect and responsibility. Love is not something to be entertained lightly, but to be embraced with the very fabric of being. How do I love thee? Let me count the ways. The ways are too deep and too numerous to be counted, but suffice it to say that real love fills the soul entirely and completes a life uncompleted.

# love is a small bird

Love is a small bird
that if we let it go will
fly and soar and hover
above us in the sky.
On release it will gain
its freedom and climb
to the clouds of lofty
heights where it will
sing of love and
freedom. If it returns it
is yours. If it does not
return it was never
meant to be. Love is
a small bird given its
freedom.

# what is it we love?

When we love, what part of the person is it we are loving? If we could isolate any one part, we would still love them. When they are not there we still love them. When they change and grow we still love them. Love is not static, nor is it dependent on the person returning our love.

What we love is the essence in that person, the vital spark that makes them human, their spirit and their essential life.

# the foundations of love

If we build on sand our house sinks. If we build love on treachery or jealousy our love will sink.

**If we build on a foundation of rock and with good stone our house will survive for centuries.**

If we build our love on trust, care and consideration, and with the good stone of mutual respect and esteem, our love will last forever. If we furnish our house with cheap furniture we will be uncomfortable and discontent. If we furnish our love with tasteful nurture and care we will be both comfortable and enriched.

Published by MQ Publications Limited
12 The Ivories 6-8 Northampton Street London N1 2HY
Tel: 020 7359 2244 / Fax: 020 7359 1616
e-mail: mail@mqpublications.com


Cover design: The Big Idea
Interior design: Bet Ayer
Cover image: Grace Carlon, Flowers & Foliage
Interior images: © Digital Vision
Series Editor: Elizabeth Carr

ISBN: 1-84072-231-2

1 3 5 7 9 0 8 6 4 2



Printed in Italy

## Note on the CD

The music that accompanies this book has been specially commissioned from composer David Baird. Trained in music and drama in Wales, and on the staff of the Welsh National Opera & Drama company, David has composed many soundtracks for both the theater and radio.

The CD can be played quietly through headphones while relaxing or meditating on the text. Alternatively, lie on the floor between two speakers placed at equal distances from you. Try and center your thoughts, and allow the soundtrack to wash over you and strip away the distracting layers of the outside world.